The Little Book of Big Wisdom for Difference Makers

Maryln Appelbaum

Appelbaum Training Institute
Houston, Texas

Printed in the United States of America
Signature Book Printing, www.sbpbooks.com
ISBN 0-9777189-8-0

Appelbaum Training Institute
Houston, Texas

About the Author

MARYLN APPELBAUM is well-known internationally as an outstanding authority on children, education, and families. She has Master's Degrees in both Psychology and Education and completed her doctoral studies in both education and psychology. She has worked as a teacher, an administrator, and a therapist and has been a consultant throughout the United States. She has written many "how to" books geared exclusively for educators and parents. She has been interviewed on television and radio talk shows and has been quoted in newspapers including U.S.A. Today. She owns a seminar training company, Appelbaum Training Institute, with her son, Marty Appelbaum, and they and their speakers train educators all over the world. Maryln's influence impacts the entire globe with her thoughts for the day that go out to thousands of educators via e-mail all over the world. Her strategies have been implemented in schools across the world successfully. There is not a day that goes by that someone does not contact her at Appelbaum Training Institute to tell her "thank you." Those "thank you's" come from teachers, administrators, parents, and students whose lives have been impacted by Maryln.

Acknowledgements

I am so grateful for all those in our offices at Appelbaum Training Institute who helped with this book. My son Marty Appelbaum continually inspires me and is an awesome partner and speaker. He found the way to get the thoughts in this book out daily to subscribers all over the world. Dave Mahavier is my great designer for the cover of this book and other books I have written. Special thanks go to Becky Walters who edited all the thoughts and continues to edit them daily so we can send them out to you in e-mails.

Sign up to get Maryln's thoughts for the day that inspired this book at www.atiseminars.org

More Books by Maryln Appelbaum

167 Strategies for Excellence
No More Battles with Strong Willed Children
No More Biting
No More Hitting
No More Tantrums
No More Tattling
How to Handle the Hard to Handle Child
How to Listen so Kids Will Talk
How to Talk so Kids Will Listen
How to Teach Kids to Follow Rules
Enter the Joyful World of Children
How to Build a Powerful Team
Stress Solutions for Children

Please call 1 800-23-CHILD or visit Appelbaum Training Institute, www.atiseminars.org to order books or to bring Maryln or one of the Appelbaum Training Institute speakers to you.

Dedication

This book is dedicated to the difference makers in this world.

Introduction

This book had very simple beginnings. It all started with an idea. I had a grandchild who was struggling in school, and I started sending him little notes each day - notes of inspiration. He loved them. It inspired me to write more. I started writing them for our company's employees. The strategies, tips, and inspirational stories started to get passed on, and soon audience members began receiving them after attending conferences. People told me they were saving them and putting them in notebooks to read when they needed an inspiration. Readers asked me to please put the thoughts into a book. This book is the result. You inspired me to write it.

Every day is a new opportunity to help children. Every day is an opportunity to leave them feeling just a little bit better about themselves than before they were in your presence. Every day is a chance to make a difference. That is what this book is all about— it is a book for you, the difference makers in the world. Together, we all CAN and WILL make this world a better place for children.

Never underestimate the power of one.

It took only one person to be persistent and invent the light bulb. It takes only one to declare war between nations. It takes only one to write a book that becomes a bestseller and influences millions. It takes only one teacher to see something within a student that is good and wake up that sleeping goodness to change the child for the better. Every President has had a teacher along the way that said, "You can do it." You have the opportunity to be the "power of one" for students.

Make every new lesson like an invitation to a party.

One of the most important parts of teaching something new to students is the introduction. Think of the introduction as a party invitation. It needs to be enticing, enthusiastic, and fun. It also needs some brief details about what will be happening at the party—enough to make people want to come—enough to make students want to learn what you will be teaching.

Use the paper clip trick to foster kindness.

Have a Kindness Jar in the room that is totally empty. Every time a student does an "Act of Kindness" – a good deed, put a paper clip into the Kindness Jar. The goal is to fill up the jar. Acts of Kindness include sharing, not interrupting, and helping another person in the class. Discuss these at the end of the class as you fill the jar with paper clips. Once the Kindness Jar is full, have a Class Kindness Celebration. The class can help decide what you will do to celebrate. Then start a new jar next to the first one. Have fun building a kindness curriculum for your class.

Use "Wait Cards."

When students want your attention, they often blurt out and interrupt the entire class. Use Wait Cards. When a student needs you, hand the student a Wait Card. This means that you will return to the student as soon as you finish what you are doing. It is a great way to acknowledge that you noticed the student without disrupting your class.

A great tool for tattlers and complainers is the "Sounds Like…" Approach.

There are some students who are chronic tattlers or complainers. It is important not to reinforce that behavior. A great tool to use is the "Sounds Like …" Approach. It validates the student's feelings, yet does not create a situation in which you are the Fixer of the problem. Here are some examples: "Sounds like that made you angry." "Sounds like that made you sad." The student will usually nod in agreement and be glad to have been acknowledged and heard. It also enables you to hear the student so that if it is something urgent like a student being bullied, you can step in and help the student.

***The more teachers care,
the more they have the courage to dare.***

It takes courage to constantly strive to find new and better answers for reaching children. It is easy to reach those who come in eager to learn. Those who come into classrooms with attitudes are the challenge. Today, look beyond appearances to find "soft spots" in those students. Perhaps you will discover something about that child's background, a hobby, a sibling, or an admired hero, to talk about. The more you connect, the less you correct, and the more students are ready to learn.

Have a Treasure Basket for when students need self-control.

Students need to learn self-control. Have a "Treasure Basket" in the classroom for this purpose. When students are upset, they go to the special place in the room that has the Treasure Basket, sit down, and remove an item that helps them become calm. The Treasure Basket has items like photos of "Treasured People" that the students choose. These people can be family members, teachers, or heroes. There are also other calming items, books, affirmations that are calming, stuffed animals, and even stress balls.

Someone has to be in charge of your classroom.
If you don't take charge, the students will!

A classroom is like a ship at sea. The ship has a captain to guide it and make sure the ship stays on course. Within that ship, there are many opportunities for other forms of leaders as well as opportunities to enjoy the ship. So too must the classroom have a leader to guide the ship on a clear course. Without that strong leader, the class will flounder. Take charge and be a strong, enthusiastic and fun leader for your classroom.

***Look at the cup half full today,
rather than half empty.***

When looking at students, it's often easier to see their faults rather than their strengths. Think of at least 3 positives about your most difficult student. Build on those strengths. The goal is to build on the strengths and watch them expand and grow. In so doing, you are helping that student to discover the strengths within. Magnify the strengths, and minimize the weaknesses until they are gone. You hold the future in your hands.

***Children are like roses that thrive
when loved and tended.***

Roses can grow by themselves, but they may not really thrive. There may be weeds. They may never reach full bloom. They may have different plant diseases. They need the caring, loving touch of a gardener. You get to work in a garden every day. It is a garden of children. They need to be tended to grow straight and tall, to fully blossom. They need tending when they go off the path. They need to be checked regularly to make sure there is nothing interfering with their thriving. They need the sunshine and water and plant food of your caring.

Put objects in "Time Away."

Sometimes there are problems with an object in the room. It can be a pencil sharpener that students use more than necessary that disrupts the class. It can be an object that children fight over. Remove the item. Put it in a special place, "Time Away." Set some boundaries on using the item before it is returned.

Remember the "Appelbaum Rule of 3."

Every time you say something and then do not follow through, the child will engage in the misbehavior at least 3 more times, thinking you will not follow through again. It is important to not say anything unless you feel strong enough to follow through. Take strength in knowing that children need you. They need you to be someone they can respect, someone who is kind and caring, and also strong enough to follow through.

***Children who have people that care about them,
are rich children.***

There are children whose parents have lots of money, yet they are impoverished children. There are children who live in socioeconomic poverty, yet they are rich children. The child who has someone that truly cares and will go the extra mile is a rich child. You cannot alter the home life of the children in your care, but you can see it to that each child experiences riches in your class.

A problem is a chance for you to do your best.

Call problems "opportunities." It changes the entire picture from a negative situation to a more positive one. The child who formerly was thought of as a "problem" now becomes an opportunity for you to reach. This is the child who really needs help. Take the opportunity to create a better world for this child and all the children you reach.

***Teach children signals to use
when they don't understand a concept.***

Children often do not know how to express their feelings appropriately. Feelings are natural. It is often the way they are expressed that can be inappropriate. For example, children who do not understand something, may act badly rather than have others think they are dumb. These children need to learn an appropriate way to say, "I don't understand. I need help." They can be taught to use words. However, this can be embarrassing for some children. In this case, teach them signals. An example of a signal is to have children touch their ear lobes until help arrives.

Collaboration is all about creating relationships.

It does take "a village to raise a child." Teamwork is essential. Just like a team cannot win a ballgame without consulting and working together and communicating, neither can children's lives be impacted in positive ways without teamwork. Take time to build teams with parents and with others who are involved in the care and education of students.

Procrastination is the enemy of accomplishment.

Taking action is the only way to accomplish anything. All the goals in the world will remain only goals without the action. Take action today to do something that will help make this world a better place for children. There are not that many chances, so take advantage of them all.

It is all in how you say it.

Choose words carefully to foster communication and understanding. For example, it can be embarrassing for a child when asked: "Is there anything you didn't understand?" Instead, you can say, "Is there anything I can help clarify?" The goal is to always enhance esteem in the child. Words can be esteem-builders or esteem-droppers.

Life is not like a computer.

Working with children means being careful with what you say and do at all times. Their minds do not only learn what you teach, but they also learn to copy attitudes, words, and acts. It is not like having a computer where you can simply hit the Control, Alt, and Delete buttons and start over. The page cannot be erased. Words can have a lasting effect. Be careful what you say. You are a difference maker.

Teach students to push the pause button.

Students are very familiar with the remote controls found on television. Have one in your room. Explain that when they are upset and feel like they may lose control, they can get the remote control, and find the pause button. They hold the pause button down and take deep breaths until they are calm again. Once they are calm, they hit "play," and return to their work in the classroom.

***Teach children how to express their
feelings appropriately.***

Most people know how to express joy. They smile and laugh.
Many know how to express love with a caring look, a hug, and
words like "I love you." Emotions children need to learn how to
express are anger, fear, and sadness. They need to understand
that these are normal emotions. Teach them to use their words to
express these feelings.

How to protect and help children when war is occurring in the world.

Newscasts sometimes have some pretty frightening events. This can have a profound effect on children. Children are affected by the way the adults in their lives feel. Just as they can "catch" moods of enthusiasm from a teacher, they can also "catch" fear and worry and anger. Here are some things you can do:

1. Acknowledge the feelings of the child. "Sounds like you are scared."
2. Have younger children draw what they are feeling.
3. Have older children journal.
4. Do not deny the seriousness of the situation.
5. Do offer hope. This is very important.

6. Keep a routine. Routines help children feel more secure.
7. Limit media, most especially the news in front of children. It can increase their anxiety and stress.
8. Children will feel more in control by taking positive actions. Students make and send things to those in the military.
9. Find opportunities to have fun. Children need to have times to be silly.
10. Create even more opportunities for movement. Build them into the day. Moving around reduces stress.

Stay focused on the present, on making a difference for children. You are a difference maker.

Have eye candy in your classroom.

Teachers spend lots of time making bulletin boards and ensuring that rooms look nice for children. Take some time to add something that makes YOU feel good. It can be a picture of someone you love, a calendar with a fun vacation you would like to take featured on the pages, or an object that has special meaning for you. This is your very own "eye candy" to make your days better too.

Everyday with children is an investment in the future.

Some people invest in stocks, bonds, or real estate. Every day that you teach, you are making deposits into the greatest bank of all—children, the future of the world.

"A flower can shatter a stone."

John Denver made a great song called, "The Flower that Shatters the Stone." It is a song about love and caring and the difference that it makes. That is what you have the opportunity to do with your words. Some students come into school hardened like thick, heavy stones. Your persistent and firm caring can gently shatter those stones. Just as waves on the beach change rocks into sand, you create waves that can change those hard stones into wonderful, engaged and enthusiastic learners.

Have a Laugh Sign.

Laughter is a great tool in the classroom. The more fun you will have, the more fun children have. Make a sign that says "laugh." Whenever you hold the sign up, children stop whatever they are doing and laugh. If you see students getting restless, hold up the sign. If there is a child in the room becoming angry, hold up the sign. If you sense that the atmosphere is too serious, and you want to make it lighter, hold up the sign.If the students are preparing for a test and are stressed, hold up the sign. Laughter is a great de-stressor.

Look for the silver lining.

Even on days that are cloudy and if you look hard enough, you can see the sunshine and the silver lining around the clouds. Life also can have its challenges, and you sometimes have to look beyond appearances to find the silver lining and the sunshine. It is the same with your classrooms. Some children come into the classrooms covered with "clouds" covering up the sunshine. It is your awesome task to help them uncover the clouds and let the sunshine in.

Make offices to block distractions.

There are some students who are easily distracted. This is easily solved by creating offices for those students. Make an "office" by taking two beige office file folders and putting them together so that they make a "standing office." Students who are easily distracted get out their office and place it around their work space to block out distractions.

Walk with confidence.

Children can sense whether or not you are a "take charge type person." If they perceive weakness, they may take advantage of you. Start with your posture and your walk. Stand up tall, and put confidence into your step. The more you believe in yourself, the more your students will believe in you and what you say.

Light up your classroom.

You are the light bulb for your classroom. Yes, there are lights in the ceiling, but you, are the sparkplug that has the ability to light up the minds and hearts of the students. Your smile, your positive encouraging words, your enthusiasm, and your firm commitment to making a difference in the lives of your students, are all keys to lighting up their worlds.

Keep it simple.

Students sometimes do not follow through because they do not understand the directions. Here are some tips for giving directions to students:

1) Be brief. State what needs to be said in as few words as possible.
2) Be clear. Make sure that students really understand what you are saying.
3) Be enthusiastic.
4) Have positive expectations. Expect that directions will be followed.
5) Tell students the benefit to be found in following the directions.

Create a Communication Station.

Set up a warm and cozy place in which to communicate with your students one-on-one. This is a place that students feel safe to talk and to be heard. When a student wants to talk to you, the student sits down in the Communication Station. The student goes there when there is a problem. The problem can be anything from the student not understanding something you are teaching, hurt feelings, or problems with other students. It is a safe place. Have rules about the Communication Station. For example, the student can only go there during certain times of the day. Only one student can go at a time. If you cannot meet with the child when the child is sitting there, you will give the child an "Appointment Card" with a time in which you will meet with the student. This is a great vehicle for getting to know your students and their needs. Communication is the key to connecting, and the more you connect, the less you correct.

Put yourself in the student's shoes.

Put yourself in the shoes of students who find learning difficult. Think of ways to reach them so that they grasp what you are teaching. It is not one size fits all. Every student learns differently. It is not a question of what the student CAN learn; it is more of a question of finding the WAY the student learns.

Put your oxygen mask on first.

When you board an airplane, you hear announcements. You are told that in the event of a problem, oxygen masks will come down. You are to put your oxygen mask on first before putting it on any children. Once you are safe, there is a better chance that you will be able to help any children. Take care of yourself. Get enough sleep. Eat healthy. Take time in the evenings to do things that nurture you. The more you take care of yourself, the more you will be able to give to your students.

Allow children to soar to success.

Here is a story. A youth found a cocoon and took it home. After several days, he saw the butterfly inside the cocoon struggling to come out. It struggled and struggled and struggled. The youth could not stand watching this struggle, so he got a pair of scissors and cut a little hole in the cocoon to help. The butterfly did emerge, but it came out with deformed wings and a swollen stomach and could not fly. The butterfly had needed its struggle because part of that struggle would have helped the butterfly's fluid in the stomach to go into beautiful wings.

The moral: Never do for a child what a child can do alone. Allow the child to soar to success.

Your words make a difference.

It just takes one kind sentence to change a child's day from feeling like everything is wrong, and the world is a gray place to sunshine skies. Sunshine skies are made out of words of encouragement, words of hope, and words of caring.

The Gift that Keeps Giving

You are the gift that keeps giving for your students. You are there for them almost every day, through inclement weather, through fatigue, through all of your own personal life's ups and downs. For some of your students, you may be the only one in their lives that is always consistent, always there, always caring. You are truly the gift that keeps giving. Thanks for what you do. You do make a difference.

Patience and Perseverance:
Key Qualities for Teachers

Disappointments with students are inevitable. The important thing is not to give up. When a student with whom you have been working lets you down, think about it as meaning that you have to respond with something else to help boost that student back up. Ultimately, it is up to the student to do the work, but you are the motivator, the coach behind the scenes that can cheer that student on to do better. You can do it. You are a difference maker.

Nothing succeeds like success.

Help each of your students feel successful at something they do in the classroom. Some students become accustomed to feeling like failures. They develop learned helplessness and think that is all they can do. Failure breeds more failures. Plant rays of hope by helping students to be successful in something they are learning. Success truly does breed success.

Be careful what you think.

It can be tough some days when working with students. It is important to keep a positive attitude on those tough days because for some children, you are the one who can help transform their lives. Start with being careful with what you think. Your thoughts become your attitudes. Your attitudes become your words. Your words become your actions. Your actions become your habits. Your habits become not only your destiny, but help shape the destiny of those you teach. The moral is to have great thoughts. You are a difference maker.

Proximity is powerful.

This is a simple yet powerful strategy. When students are just starting to misbehave or are already in the act of misbehaving, simply walk over to them as you teach and continue teaching while standing there. The children become quiet because you are in close proximity.

You never know the difference you make.

Here is a personal story that touched me so deeply that I wanted to share it with you. I was at a gathering, and a woman who looked vaguely familiar came up to me. She told me her name and said that I had her son in my school when he was younger. She wanted me to know that her son was nearly finished with college and was graduating with straight A's as an engineer. She reminded me that when I took her son into my school, he had been in another school in which they could not work with him. He had been labeled, in her words, "retarded." That is when she brought him to my school. That was in the late 70's. I individualized a program of instruction for him, and he thrived. More than anything, I gave him and the family hope , hope that he COULD achieve. She thanked me with tears in her eyes, and I have to share that I too had tears in my eyes as she told me this story.

This is what we each can do for each of our students, individualize, and give them hope. Give their families hope. It's a great gift.

You build bridges to the future.

This world has never needed you more. Your work is an important key to building better futures for children. Every child you influence has the potential to positively influence others. The children you teach potentially can become important world leaders tomorrow, and it could all begin with a dream that you planted within a child's mind and heart. The future belongs to all who believe in the possibility of fulfilled dreams. Teach your children to dare to dream, to reach further than they have ever reached before, and to strive always for success. You can do it. You are a teacher and a difference maker.

Hook them in the first minutes.

Students come into the classroom thinking about all kinds of things. They may be worrying about a family member, angry about something that happened, or thinking about a friend. Your goal is not to STOP children from thinking, but instead to START them thinking about the class they are in and the work they are doing. Hook them in the first minutes. Do something totally unexpected. Play a song. Wear a funny hat. Have an interesting game for them to do! When you "hook them," you can teach them.

"I have a dream."

Martin Luther King said these powerful words. I too have a dream. I dream of the day when teachers will be acknowledge, honored, and respected for the key roles they play in building the future. I dream of the day when parents will look at you who work with children and realize how important your work and your influence are in the lives of their children. They will respect you and want to work together as a team on behalf of their children. I dream of the day when lawmakers will respect you, the work you do, and the difference you make in the lives of children, and hear your collective voice before making decisions that influence your lives and the lives of children.

I dream of the day when the corporate world will acknowledge you for the key role you play in preparing their future employees. I dream of the day when you will walk inside a room filled with people and when someone says, "What do you do," you respond, "I'm a teacher," and they will applaud you and thank you for the important work you do.

I dream of the day when students will come into your schools and classrooms with newfound respect passed on from their families and salute you as a huge difference-maker in their lives.

Thank you Martin Luther King. Your words inspired us to dream too. You inspired us to dream about the future as we build a better world for children.

Fill your teapot.

All week you give and give and give. You give to students, to co-workers, to parents of your students, and to creating new lessons to be learned. Just like a teapot left on a burner can burn-out once empty, so too, can you burn-out. Your teapot can become empty when you give, give, give, and don't take time to fill yourself back up.

Start now to fill your teapot. Fill it up with the smiles from students with whom you do succeed. Fill it up with words of acknowledgement and appreciation you hear from co-workers and friends. Fill it up with doing some special things for yourself like taking time for a long bath, reading a good book, going to a movie, or sharing a meal with loved ones and having great communication.

You are a difference maker. Take care of yourself so you can keep making a difference in the lives of others.

Use "I Need" talk.

It is much more powerful to use "I talk" than to use "You talk."
Here are a few examples:
YOU TALK: "You never listen."
I NEED TALK: "I need you to listen when I speak."

YOU TALK: "You're rude and disrespectful."
I NEED TALK: "I need you to speak to me in a respectful tone."

When you use "I talk," there's a greater likelihood that students
will listen. It is not about what they are doing wrong, as much as
what you need them to do that is RIGHT. It is a more respectful
way of asking for what you want and ensuring that you get it.

The words you use and the tone with which you speak make a
huge difference.

When you smile…

I want to share a very personal story with you. Two weeks ago, I got a call that my mom had to be taken to the hospital. I immediately flew to be with her in Ohio. She was 91, and her body simply started to shut down. I got to the hospital through a blizzard. It was immediately apparent that my mom was not doing well. Her eyes were shut, and I said, "Mom, it's Maryln. I'm here." She opened her eyes, recognized me and smiled that sweet smile that she always had. She immediately closed her eyes again. I knew she was happy to see me, but she had also seen the tears in my eyes, and she could feel with a mother's love, the huge ache I had in my heart at the thought of losing her.

It became very obvious that she wanted to tell me something because she became very agitated trying to talk, but her voice was not working, and she could not speak. I felt so helpless, so I started to pray that I would understand what she wanted to say to

me. I kept talking to her, soothing her, and praying with her. Minutes ticked on, and I just kept talking while she moved frantically trying to talk. Suddenly, I decided to sing to her. I sang to her one of her favorite songs, "When you're smiling, when you're smiling, the whole world smiles with you. When you're laughing, when you're laughing, the sun comes shining through." My mom totally changed. She became calm and peaceful as I sang. Suddenly, I knew what she wanted to tell me. I said to her, "That's it. That's what you wanted to tell me. You saw me crying, and you wanted me to remember to smile too. You want me to remember to laugh and enjoy life too. I'll do it Mom. I'll always remember. I'll tell your grandchildren, your great grandchildren. I'll tell the people who work with children. I'll remind everyone to smile and laugh and enjoy life and what they do." And so today, my friends, I am telling you to remember to smile and

laugh and enjoy your work and your life. Your smile can warm up those you influence like a ray of sunshine. That is what my mom did for me and for others in her life. That is what you can do too.

My mom quietly and peacefully passed away a short time later. I have been mourning her, and I cannot say that I do not cry when I think about her. But I also know she left me a legacy of love, a smile that lit up a room, and I remember her last "words" to me, and those words apply to all of us who make a difference in the lives of children. Spread that smile of yours. Spread joy and sunshine into the lives of your students. Your smiles live on in the hearts of your children, just as my mom does in me and my family. You are a difference maker.

"If you hear my voice…."

A great way to get the attention of students is to say, "If you hear my voice," and follow it with a set of instructions. Here are some examples of different ways to use this simple and effective strategy:

"If you hear my voice, clap your hands two times."

"If you hear my voice, blink your eyes three times."

"If you hear my voice, say, "Hurray."

The more students actually listen to what you have to say, the more engaged they are, and the more engaged they are, the more they can learn.

Involve the student in a solution for problem behavior.

This is a powerful technique that works for all ages. It is effective because it empowers the student, while still making it clear that the behavior cannot reoccur. Tell the student what the problem behavior is. (He or she really already knows!) Then say, "I need your help with this behavior." Say, "I need YOU to tell me what WILL work." Give the child time to think about it and come up with a solution.

I have used this with children of all ages, but I will always remember the first time I used it. It was with a student who was misbehaving over and over again. He had done this with other teachers, and now he was doing it with me. I had tried everything

to get the misbehaviors to stop. I finally met with him one-to-one. I said to him, "I have tried many strategies and nothing seems to work. I need your help! I want you to take time to come up with something that will work." He thought and thought, and he finally said, "Well, I could tie a string around my finger, and it could even be a red string, but that won't work!!!" Then his voice got real low and deep, and he said, "The only thing that will really work is a reminder note. Put it on my desk when you see me getting out of line." I had him write the reminder card. Not only was it effective, but it was also the beginning of a great relationship with me and this student.

You are part of a caring connection.

Wherever you are, as you are reading this, know that that you are not alone. You may be alone in your classroom, but you are not alone in the important work that you do. All over the world, there are people who do what you do—people who strive to make a difference in the lives of students. When you add all of the great people together who work on behalf of children, you have a team—a world team! Each person on that team makes a difference. Together, this team that you are a part of builds a better world for children. You are a difference maker!

Teach children how to express anger appropriately.

Almost everyone learns how to express love. It is expressed through hugs, words, smiles, or special gifts of the heart. However, few people are taught how to express anger appropriately. Everyone at some time or another has felt anger. It is a normal emotion. Teach students how to express anger appropriately. Have them use words, like "I am angry," rather than fists. It is important that they learn not to speak in anger, but to wait until they are calm. Words can hurt. Teach them tools like deep breathing to cool down. This is an awesome tool that will last them their entire lives—the ability to express themselves appropriately.

You just never know the difference you make.

I want to share with you a story about one of my students. Jenna*
was a really tough student I had early in my teaching career. She
was taller than any other child in my class, very slim, had a long
dark ponytail, and huge hardened, very dark eyes. She was an
angry child, would talk back when asked to do anything, and
treated me and all the other students with disrespect. I checked
into her background and learned that her dad had left before she
was born, and her mom left a few years later. She was being
raised by an elderly grandmother. The grandmother was worn
out. She felt like a failure because of what had happened with
her daughter, and now had just given up on Jenna.

I resolved that I would help Jenna. I set aside a special time each
day to meet with her alone for five minutes one-to-one. I told her
that I wanted to get to know her. I mostly listened as she talked.
In the early sessions, she mostly vented anger. She talked about
how she hated her mother, her dad, and even her grandmother.
Slowly she began to trust me. She said she had no friends. She

told me she really didn't know how to get friends. I asked her if she would like me to pair her up with a "learning buddy." She thought about that for nearly a week before she told me to go ahead. I did, and soon, she and her learning buddy became friends. It was amazing to watch Jenna that school year. I kept meeting with her daily. Her eyes became brighter, and she went from being an unhappy, sullen, angry child to a really happy child. What a joy! Eventually, she moved on to another grade and another school.

One day, many years later I was leading a seminar, and an attractive tall woman came up to me and introduced herself. It was Jenna! She was now a teacher, and she loved her work! She had on her great smile. She thanked me for taking the time to be there for her when she really needed it. She said she became a teacher so that she could do the same thing for other children. You just never know the difference that you make each day in the lives of your children.

The more you give, the more you receive.

Teaching is about giving so much. You give to the students, to families, to the lessons you plan, and to the projects you make. But you also receive so much. You get to watch a student progress from knowing little to knowing much. You receive the smiles, the hugs, the words of the students and their families. One smile from a student who had been tough to reach, can fill your day with sunshine of the heart. Yes, it's true. The more you give, the more you receive.

Verbal sunshine is found in kind words.

When you say something kind to a student, it is like spreading verbal sunshine. You may be the first person to do this for the student. Today, as you go through your day, spread verbal sunshine not only to the students you teach, but to all those you encounter— your co-workers, your family, your friends, and your neighbors. You may not be able to affect the weather outside, but you sure can affect the "weather" inside the hearts and minds of those around you!

Light up the darkness.

One very small candle adds light to a dark room. One lit match can light the way for those who are lost. One small light bulb can bring light where there was no light before. You are like a light bulb for your students. One smile, one kind sentence, one statement like, "I believe in you," can transform a child's life from darkness to light.

I remember meeting a man who was a successful financial planner for many Hollywood figures. He told me that he did poorly all through school. He barely passed all subjects. In high school he played football. He was in danger of being booted off the team because of failing grades. He told me that his coach said, "Ken,

I believe in you. You can do better." He said no one had ever said this to him in his entire life. Those words changed his life. He started to think he could do better, and he did. He started working harder. His grades improved. He went on to college. He became a success in his profession and always remembered those words his coach said to him, "I believe in you. You can do better."

You can do this too. You can light up a student's world with your words. You are a difference maker.

Use power listening skills.

Communication is much more than words. It is about being able to listen and also to speak in a manner that makes others want to listen. In order to connect with students, take time to listen. This is especially true with children who have problems. Set aside a special time to meet one-to-one. When you listen, focus your entire attention on the student. Nod your head as you listen so the child knows you are paying attention. Use power listening words: "Ah…," "Really!" and "I would like to hear more." This is a gift you can give not only to your students but to all of those in your life—the gift of listening without interrupting and without attempting to solve the problem. It is empowering.

Make more deposits than withdrawals.

When a bank checking account has more withdrawals than deposits, it gets insufficient funds. A huge cycle begins with more and more checks bouncing and more and more late fees. It can become nearly impossible to bail out.

Life is like a bank account. Each day there are opportunities for deposits or withdrawals. A deposit is something that is nurturing, that enhances the person. A withdrawal is something that depletes the person. Some of the students you teach have had so many withdrawals that a cycle has been set up so that they believe they will fail. They do not believe they can do anything right. They have come to expect that they cannot learn or that they cannot behave. These children need deposits. That is where you come in. Every day you have a new opportunity to make deposits into your students' accounts. You are a difference maker.

There is much beauty to be found in a box of crayons.

An open box of crayons contains many colors. Each color has its own unique beauty. Some of the crayons in the box may be shorter, some longer, some may have pointy tips, and some have been used so much that they are more rounded. Some of the names of colors are simple one syllable names; others are more difficult to say. When these crayons are used together, they create a beautiful drawing. Your classroom is the same. Every child is like one of those crayons, unique and special. Together, with your help, your school year can become a beautiful painting as you unite your class into a "we" instead of a "me" classroom.

Use "put-ups!"

A "put-up" is the opposite of a "put-down." Put-downs are critical words that make children feel badly. Children use "put-downs" often in their communication. They may learn to do this from watching television or from other children. The problem with "put-downs" is that they are cumulative. After awhile, the child who hears them begins to believe them. The more a child thinks that he or she is bad, the more the child will act the part. "Put-ups" are words that boost students to success. Teach your students to use "put-ups"—words that make others feel better. You will be contributing to fostering the esteems of students! Wouldn't it be a better world if political leaders and media used more "put-ups" than "put-downs?" It all has to begin somewhere. Your classroom is the beginning of building a better more respectful world for everyone. You are a difference maker.

Your actions speak louder than your words.

Children "read" your body language. Have you ever traveled to a foreign country where you do not speak the language? You may not understand the words, but you "read" what people are saying. You watch their facial expressions. You watch their mannerisms. It is the same with the students you teach. They "read" your facial expressions and your body language. They can tell whether you like them by your actions—by your total body language. Do you smile broadly to welcome a child? Do you look like you are happy to be in the classroom? Today and everyday, have them watch you and "read" the language of caring, concern, and compassion.

Children are like seeds planted deeply in the soil.

In some climates, winter means there is a blanket of snow on the ground. But deep underneath the snow, seemingly dormant lies plants for spring—grass, shrubbery, and flowers. Everything is waiting for warmth and sunshine to emerge into blossoming plants. It is a complete transformation of beauty. In the same way, you can have a complete transformation in your toughest child. The child may be frozen into negativity, but with your compassion, the negativity can melt away, and the child can blossom. You are a difference maker.

Put yourself in the child's shoes.

There was once a girl who was raised in a home in which her parents spoke no English. When she started Kindergarten, she had no idea what the teacher was saying. She felt lost and frightened. Another kindergarten child came up to her and helped her. He showed her what to do and when to do it. Her fear left. She understood what she needed to do, and she had a new friend too. That child was me!

When you are teaching, you may have children who do not understand you. It can be because of a language barrier, or it may be because of a different learning style. Some children may be very bright, but they are visual learners so when you give them auditory instructions, they just don't get it! Put yourself in the shoes of the children in your classroom. Seek to understand them and to reach them. You can do it. You are a difference maker.

There are 1440 chances.

Every day you receive 1440 minutes. They are yours to spend as you want. Those are 1440 opportunities – minutes in your life to be a difference maker—to be that someone that makes a huge difference in the lives of children, your own family, and friends. You can "spend" those 1440 minutes, but you cannot "save" them. What you can save, are the memories. That is what your students can save too. Give those in your life some special memories that they can save forever. They are precious gifts that they can open on days they need those memories.

The sun can come out after the rain.

There are times in most parts of the world when there is a lot of rain. There may be storms with thunder and lightening. In some children's lives there have been storms. The storms may not have been caused by rain, but by things you cannot see—a home that is constantly transient, abuse, addiction, extreme poverty or even extreme overindulgence. You cannot control outside forces like storms, and often there is very little you can do about the child's home life, but there is something you can do even in the midst of the storms, and that is to take time for students who need it the most. A great strategy for children who are unconnected, disruptive, defiant, is to take only three minutes a day—three uninterrupted minutes, to be with that child, to listen to the child talk, to find out the child's likes and interests, to connect. Do this for three consecutive weeks. Watch how the child responds. It is true that the more you connect, the less you correct. You will be helping children have some sunshine in their lives. You are a difference maker.

There is a difference between fair and equal.

The question often comes up, "Is it fair—is it okay to do something for one student and not for the others?" Here is a story to help illustrate the answer to that important question.

A doctor had three patients in his waiting room. One had a cut that was bleeding profusely. Another patient had had a high temperature for nearly a week. The third patient had a really bad cough. The doctor came out and handed each patient two aspirins. He treated them all equally. But was that fair? In reality, each patient needed their own special treatment.

So too it is with children. Each child in your class is unique and special. Each child needs whatever it takes to help that student succeed and learn. Tell your students, "I want you each to succeed. You each can do it. I will do whatever it takes for each one of you to make sure that happens." Then do it! You are a difference maker!!!

Use the strings you have left, to make beautiful music.

There is a story told about a famous violinist that is very inspiring. Itzhak Perlman had polio as a child and wears leg braces and uses crutches as a result. He had an amazing thing happen at one of his concerts at Lincoln Center in New York. He walked onto the stage slowly because of his crutches and braces, and sat down in a chair. He then put down his crutches and took off his braces. He began to play. Just as he finished the first few bars, one of the strings on his violin broke with a loud snap. He only had three strings left. Everyone waited for him to put his leg braces back on and leave the stage, but he did not. Instead, he closed his eyes, waited a minute, and then signaled the conductor to start. Up to that time, it was thought that it was impossible to play a symphonic work with three strings, but Itzhak Perlman refused to know that. He kept modulating and changing as he played. He made beautiful music! When he finished, there was total silence and then a huge

outburst of applause and a standing ovation. When it became quiet, he was asked how he did it. He told the audience, that "sometimes it is the artist's task to find out how much music you can make with what you have left."

And that is what you have to do too! You are like the artist that has to create harmony and learning—to make beautiful music with your students. They will not all be perfect. They are each different. Some may have "broken strings" of lost hope or special needs. Yet, you too, can bring out their best qualities. You do that with your patience, your kindness, your engaging teaching methods, your persistence, and with your caring. You can do it. You can make beautiful music with "the strings that are left." You are a difference maker.

Avoid power struggles.

There are some students who are argumentative and thrive on power struggles.

Here are some strategies for success with these students:

1) Do not argue, get defensive, yell, or use sarcasm.

2) Do calmly say, "Regardless" or "Nevertheless" and tell the student what it is you want or need. Use "I talk." "Regardless, I would appreciate it if you would….." or "Nevertheless, I need you to………"

3) Stay calm. Have your voice and mannerisms exude confidence and a calm manner.

4) Offer two positive choices. "You can do _____, or you can do _____." Which do you prefer to do now?"

In each scenario, you are the one who is in charge. Students need you to be in charge, to be consistent, and to provide structure. You are their teacher. You are a difference maker.

Motivation is an important key to success.

Sometimes, something someone says has a profound effect. That happened to me when I took my first college class in psychology. My instructor, who had his PhD in psychology, told us about his graduating class. He said that the student who had the highest grades did so well because he had more of one magic ingredient than the other students. It was not his IQ, which was actually lower than the other students. It was MOTIVATION. He was determined to succeed, and so he did. What an important message that was for me and for all who teach. Students come into the classrooms with diverse learning styles, diverse IQ's, and many with their own special needs. Yet, each student can still be motivated to succeed. It is an important key to learning success.

Teach children to be overcomers.

To overcome means to "come over to" something different. Many times students get stuck in behaviors, in patterns, that keep them from learning. Instead of focusing on what they are doing that is inappropriate, teach them new more appropriate behaviors. For example, there are some students that do not ever learn from consequences. They still keep doing the same thing over and over again. Teach these students new appropriate behaviors to replace the old ones. Teach them to never give up! That is a lasting legacy of love you can leave each of your students.

Avoid the "No, No, No, Yes, game."

It is easy to get hooked into a game with students. They ask you for something, and you say "no." Then they ask you again and again. Eventually, they wear you down, and you say "yes." Each time that your "no" turns into a "yes," students learn that they CAN get what they want if they just hold out long enough. That is why they hold out longer and longer. It becomes a game for them, a game in which you lose, and they also lose. They lose because they are learning to engage in inappropriate behaviors to get what they want.

Be consistent. When you say something, follow through. You may have to keep saying to yourself, "I can do this. I can do this." And you can! You are a difference maker.

Fragile—Handle with Care.

There are some packages marked "fragile—handle with care." When you open these packages, you have to go through several layers of protective coverings to get to the contents. It is the same with some of the children in your care. They wear protective coverings. It is tough to get inside and see what is really there. These children need to be handled with care. If you jump right in to pull apart the coverings, you might do damage to the contents. Take your time. The protective layers will come off bit by bit as the child feels safe and secure. The treasure that is the heart of the child waits inside.

Shift into neutral and put the brakes on.

When you are driving a car and shift into neutral and put the brakes on, you cannot go forward, and you cannot go backwards. You simply stop. When you get upset with a student, it is best not to talk until you have taken time to gather your thoughts. Words can be harmful. Shift your mind into neutral rather than staying upset. Think of the child's attributes. Think of what you want to accomplish with the child. Take time to breathe! All of this may take just a few seconds. When you are ready, shift back into "Drive" and take your foot off the brakes.

Today is a great day because you are here.

Have a sign on your door that children see when they arrive. It can be "Today is a great day because you are here." Add some clip art showing welcoming hands so that children instantly know when they arrive into your classroom that they are welcome and that you are so glad they are there.

The truth is that each day becomes great with the arrival of children. The arrival of children signals the start of something great—the start of a new day in which to make a difference in their lives, and in that way, to make this world a better place.

Think of a paper clip before you speak.

If you take a paperclip and stretch it out, it can never be put back in exactly the same way as it was before it was stretched. Words can have the same effect. Your words are powerful. The words you say to a child can stretch the child forth in wonderful new directions. Your words also can influence a child in negative ways so that the child may look the same on the outside, but never again be the same on the inside. Let your words always be an inspiration to children. You are a difference maker.

Have a Dream Bench.

I remember many years ago doing two programs for a school. I was told by the administrators ahead of time that the school was in a high poverty area. There was a high rate of substance abuse by families, and that was the path that most of the children would follow. No one had ever told those children that they could dream, that they could have more. My in-services were for both the teachers and for the parents. I told them my story. I was born to parents who were new to the United States. They spoke very little English. We lived in a high poverty—high crime area in a tiny one bedroom apartment. I slept on a small chair that opened into a bed. My mom would make a huge pot of meat and vegetable soup that had to last an entire week. We used bread because it was inexpensive to fill up our stomachs when we were hungry.

Just walking to school was an experience of fear because of the neighborhood. However, there was one thing that my family gave me that we have to give to all children, and that was hope! They dreamed of better days for themselves and for me. They taught me to dream.

Have a Dream Bench in your classroom. It is a place that children can go to think about their dreams. They can share those dreams with the class at a specified time. Teach them to dare to dream, to dare to hope. Tell them stories of people who overcame adversity to make their lives better.

The Recording Mind is set on "Record."

The child's mind has a feature similar to a tape recorder that is set on "record." It records everything that happens in the child's world. Actually, "The Recording Mind" is one of the unique ways children learn. They look at the world around them and see and hear and experience images all the time. They learn to "play back" what they see. They imitate both the actions and the words of important people in their lives.

When you are working with children, it is important to remember that their minds are always on "Record." The words you say to them, and the actions you do are being recorded. Just as the mind can "Play back" negative experiences, it can also play back positive experiences. Your words like "I believe in you," can be activated for them both in the present and also for years to come when they are adults. It can help them to overcome "negative recordings." Help them always to record positive experiences. You are a difference maker.

Life can begin again.

About six months ago, I bought a really beautiful, tiny purple orchid plant on sale. It was magnificent. It had beautiful delicate flowers and for about six weeks, it made my kitchen brighter and more beautiful. When it stopped blooming, I put it outside. I watered it and kept it in a spot where it would get some shaded sunlight. It looked like it had died. I did not give up hope. I kept tending the little potted plant, watching for any signs of life. Recently, I went outside, and there was a beautiful orchid and lots of tiny new buds. The plant is back in my kitchen adding beauty and brightness.

And so it is with children. They too always need to have someone who hopes for them and believes in them, even through the darkest days. They each need to be carefully tended, observed, cared for, and one day, they too can bloom into all they can be. That is what you do. You are a difference maker. You help children blossom and flourish.

Handle with Care

Some of the children you work with may be diagnosed with special needs. Others may have special needs that have not been diagnosed. Handle these children and their families with great care. It is not easy to be the parent of a child with special needs. Go that extra mile to assure the parent. Work as a cooperative team on behalf of the child. Go that extra mile with the child to ensure that child can and does succeed. Above all, never stop believing in the child. Children and their families know when you care. They don't care how much you know until they know how much you care. You are a difference maker.

Learning is about the process.

There are often state and federal requirements that demand a "product" of test scores to show that children are learning. I don't hear much about the process of learning. Children each have their own learning process. Some children need more repetition in order to learn something. Some are quick learners and just need to hear something once, and they are ready to springboard the information into something else. Some children learn exclusively from visual examples and demonstrations while other children need hands-on to learn best. A very small percentage of learners are auditory—needing to only hear something to "get it."

ALL children however, share one huge trait in the PROCESS of learning, and that is that the more enjoyable the learning, the more they learn. Help your children enjoy the process and watch them thrive!!!

They say nothing lasts forever.

It is said that nothing lasts forever. There ARE things that last forever. They are not television sets, computers, cars, homes, or other material things. Instead, they are things given by those who care.

Here are examples from my life from those who care:

- My dad's love and fun teasing and the way he reached out to help others;
- My mom's smile and words, "When you are smiling, the whole world smiles with you."
- A teacher who believed in me at a time I needed it;
- Holding each of my own children and grandchildren in my arms that first time—is there anything in this world that can compare!!

- Hugs and love from those I love and have loved;
- Watching the looks on audience members' faces when they are having fun while learning;
- Family dinners, sharing laughter and love; and
- The feeling of joy I receive as I write these thoughts of the day for you, and hear back from you how much you enjoy them.

You probably have some wonderful caring memories that have lasted forever for you. Every day you have an opportunity to give children love and knowledge that lasts forever—that helps them to be all that they can be. Your work lasts forever in the hearts and minds of those you reach and teach.

The best outfit is FREE!

The most wonderful outfit is free! It attracts the attention of your students in positive ways. It brightens up the rooms in which you teach. Every day when you get dressed, you put on the most important piece of clothing of all—it is your attitude. Enjoy your great outfit today and the world around you will enjoy it too.

Be all you want kids to be.

Children learn not only from what you teach them, but from watching you and who you are. Do you get so busy that you don't take time for yourself? That is what children learn. Do you lose your temper? That is what kids will learn. Do you eat healthy foods? That is what kids will see and copy. Do you speak in a caring way about those important people in your life? That is what children will learn.

Do you love to learn new things? Are you an optimistic type of person? Everything you are and do, kids may copy. You are a role model at all times. Be all you want the children you teach to be.

Children are treasures!!!

Working with children is like opening up a treasure box each day. The first step in finding buried treasure is to have the willingness and desire to go on a treasure hunt. It takes time, energy, and commitment.

The second step is the search for the treasure. Working with children involves showing them how much you care—creating a safe haven. The more they sense that you care, the safer they feel to open up the treasure chests of their feelings, dreams, and hopes. The third and final step is the treasure itself. Those are the moments when children really let you into their lives and share with you. Those are moments of pure connection as you listen to the children.

Do the best you can with what you have.

There was a young boy in S. Africa, Nkosi, who was born with AIDS. His mom had died of AIDS, and he was expected to die by the time he was two years old. A woman named Gail Johnson adopted him from the home he was living in that was filled with AIDS victims. She nurtured him, and this brave little boy surprised the world by living to be 12 years old. During his short life he became a spokesman to help other children with AIDS. He gave a speech at an international conference. NPR and BBC heard about the speech and passed it on to others. At the conference Nkosi said, "Do all you can with what you have." He was a powerful voice. His memory lives on with a foundation in S.Africa called Nkosi's Haven. He did all he could with what he had.

That is what you are called to do each day—to do all you can with what you have. You not only teach children, but you create a haven for them. You are a difference maker.

Have hope.

I would like to share with you a personal story. I have a dear friend and mentor who I call "Poppa James" (90) that has had cancer. He has been in his home, in the bedroom he shared with his beloved wife who also passed away from cancer. For three days, he was mostly delirious. On the third day, I returned from out of town. On that day, I soothed him, a change was made in his medication, and prayers were said for him. That same evening, my son Marty and my granddaughter Ciara, went to visit him. My granddaughter held his hands and told him she loved him. Something dramatic happened that night. He awoke the next morning, and his mind was clear as a bell. Was it the sweet love of a child? Was it a change in his meds? Was it the prayers? Was it being surrounded by those who loved him? Whatever it was,

for that one awesome day, he still had cancer, but mentally and emotionally, he was back to being the dear sweet person that so many of us have grown to know and love. It was such a joy and seemed like such a miracle. I have a point to this story that relates to students. You don't always know for sure which tool will work, but it is important to keep trying, and hoping—and never give up. Keep hoping even when there does not seem to be any hope. Children can feel it. You cannot change some of their circumstances—things happening in the home, learning handicaps, special needs, but you can still make a profound change in the lives of your students—a change for the better so that they can learn and be all the best they can be!

There are no wrong houses.

You have all kinds of students in your classroom. You may think, "Why did I get this one?" or "I don't know if I can handle this student." Here is a story that I hope helps you realize that you and the student may be right where you are supposed to be.

I have shared with you a story about my dear friend and mentor, Poppa James. I want to share with you how I met him and his wife. Over twenty years ago, I lived for a short time in a home in Sugar Land, and had an incredible older couple as neighbors. They always smiled and often cut roses from their garden and brought them to me to brighten my home. I moved out of town, and we lost contact. When I moved back five years later, I saw their car in their driveway, and was excited to think they were

still alive. I walked up to the house and rang their doorbell. Imagine my surprise when a different elderly couple answered the door. I apologized for disturbing them and told them I saw the car and thought the former couple still lived in that home. The elderly woman, Beth, explained that they had bought the house as well as the automobile when the first couple had passed away. Her husband, James, gave a cute little click with his mouth and said, "We're not the Williams, but come on in honey, and let's all get to know each other." And that is how it all began. A week or two later, I caught a bad cold, and they came to me saying, "Here's Meals on Wheels" with homemade chicken soup and a great meal. Soon we were taking care of each other. I was there

for them through illnesses, and they were there for me. They even played a role in helping our business get started. This dear family and I spent many evenings together putting labels and stamps on brochures that were mailed to some of you reading this today. We would sit and talk about helping make this world a better place for children as we worked together. Their love accompanied every brochure. Their love still fills all the work we do. What seemed like an accident with me ringing the doorbell of people who no longer lived there, was a gift. It had a purpose. It was not the wrong house. It was the right house for me and forever changed my life.

It is the same with you and the students you have. They too are most probably in just the "right house." You have an opportunity to forever change the lives for the better of these students. It will take time and patience. You can do it. You are a difference maker.

Children need guidance.

When you look out at the stars at night, you look at the North Star to locate the other stars in the sky. When you drive in a new neighborhood, you need a compass, a map, or a GPS finder to find your location. It is the same with children. They too need guidance. This guidance comes in many forms. It is having a routine for them to follow so they always know what to expect. It is class rules. It is clear directions. Your guidance guides them through the many storms they can encounter and leads them on the path to success.

Happiness is in the small things.

There is a magic formula to being happy with your work and with your life. It is easy. It is free. It is simply being grateful for what you have right now. It is about smiling whenever you think of a certain student. It is looking up at the sunshine or at a star and feeling great to be part of this magnificent world. It is holding a child's hand and in so doing, touching the child's heart. Happiness is in the small things. Happiness is an "inside job." Start today to look around at all the things that make you smile.

You are part of a world team of difference makers.

You may be alone in a classroom, but you are not alone in the important work you do. Every day, all over the entire world people go to work to help children. Their goal is the same as your goal— to make a difference. They often do not make huge sums of money. Their rewards are in seeing the smiles on children's faces, the progress children are making, and that great day when they got through to a child who seemed unreachable. It is amazing when you think about the fact that you are all joined in purpose. You are all joined in dedication. You are all joined in being part of a movement to shape this world as it has never been shaped before. You together build the future—the future leaders of the world. If right now as you are reading this, everyone could shout, "Hurray for us," you would carry a message of your dedication across the globe.

In reality, you do shout everyday through the work you do—"I am a difference maker—part of a world team of difference makers building the future of the world."

Give instructions so that all learners understand.

I can still remember joining an exercise class. The instructor "told" us how to do an exercise. She gave long auditory directions. Then we were to do what she had just said. I stood there lost. I felt like everyone else in the entire class knew what she was talking about except me. I did not know at that time that I was a visual learner. Later, I worked up the guts to take another exercise class. The instructor told us what to do while she demonstrated it. I could see her as well as hear her. I jumped in and did what I had seen her do. Many of you also have visual learners in your classroom. Actually, the majority of learners are visual.

Here is a great way to give instructions so that all learners will understand them.

1. Have your instructions be clear and succinct—just one a time.
2. Demonstrate what it is you want done.
3. Have a visual reminder on a paper or whiteboard.
4. If you see a child looking puzzled, the child may actually be puzzled. Go over to the child and help the child follow the directions

Have fun teaching children. You are a difference maker.

Handle with care.

My 10 month old, sweet 6 ½ pound puppy Snuggles fell and broke his leg. He had to have surgery, and now he has a plate and screws in his leg and a huge splint that is longer than his leg. He went from one moment being a regular puppy to now being a puppy with special needs. He cannot get his splint wet, cannot romp around for 6-8 weeks, and has to be carefully fed his food and given water and medicine. I had to even get some special equipment to accommodate his special needs. That reminds me of the children you have in your classrooms. Some of them also have special needs. Some cannot do things for themselves. They need that extra help. They need to be nurtured and carefully tended. It is not always as easy to see the special needs like with Snuggles. They do not all wear splints on the outside, but on the inside, they too may have special needs. They may need extra

nurturing. Some children come into the classrooms not with broken legs, but with broken hearts. They do not understand why their parents are not together anymore. Some children think it is their fault. Some children miss a family member that is away. Some feel abandoned. Some are dealing with loss, the loss of a pet. Some are dealing with even bigger loss, the loss of self-esteem when they think they cannot do something that it seems everyone else can do. Handle these children with care. On the outside, they may be covering up their special needs with scowls and "walls," but on the inside, they may be shivering and scared and lonely. Take it slowly. Be gentle. Look for how you can accommodate those special needs. My little Snuggles will heal with patience, love, and caring. So too, can your children heal with your patience, love, and caring. You are a difference maker.

Be creative about taking attendance.

Taking attendance can set the tone for the classroom day. Remember, that it is best NOT to take attendance by calling out names and having the children say, "Here." This becomes boring for the students. Bored kids are more likely to misbehave.

Here are some practical and simple ways to take attendance depending on your style and the ages of the students you are teaching:

- ➤ Look at your class and then look at your seating chart. Mark whoever is absent.
- ➤ Ask the children "Who is missing today?" They will tell you.
- ➤ Have an In-Out Chart hanging on wall. Children take a clothes pin with their name on it and clip it to In-Column. For non-

readers, have a sticker next to the child's name so that the child can easily recognize his/her clothes pin.

➢ Have folders for each student up front. As children come in the classroom, they each take their folder to their seat. The remaining folders are the children who are absent.

Have fun thinking of other creative ways to take attendance. It's important to set the tone for a great learning experience for your class.

Avoid fuel-line freeze-up.

I was born in Ohio, and we had some cold icy winters. We always had to remember to have enough gas in our cars. If the fuel was low, it could freeze so that when you tried to start the car, it would not work. It was called "fuel-line freeze-up." That is the same thing that happens to some students. They get "fuel-line freeze-up." They see a test, and they cannot "start." When they finally do start taking the test, they sputter and stop over and over again. They may know the material, but they simply cannot produce results because of severe anxiety. You can reduce this anxiety by renaming tests "opportunities." Have silver opportunities for quick quizzes and gold and platinum opportunities for larger assessments.

Establish connections.

Have you ever walked into a room filled with strangers? It feels awkward. Contrast that to walking into a room filled with acquaintances – people you know and like – who also know and like you. In the latter scenario, you see faces that smile when they see you, and you hear words of greeting. It helps you to feel more comfortable and at-ease. That is exactly what students need too. There are some students that easily form connections with others. There are other students that find this difficult. Help your students establish connections. You can do this several ways. One easy way is to seat children who need a friend near someone warm and friendly. Partner a shy student with someone outgoing and caring. Break children frequently into different small groups for learning activities so that they get to know each other. Have whole group bonding activities. Take time to individually connect with your students. The more you connect, the less you correct. Have fun helping children establish connections.

Smiles inspire trust.
Trust inspires caring.
Caring inspires connection.
Connection inspires motivation to learn.
And it all starts with a smile!

Remember the elevator technique.

Your voice can be compared to an elevator. When you raise your voice, it is like pushing the button on an elevator. All the voices in the classroom go up! When you lower your voice and whisper, you are pushing the DOWN button, and all the voices in the classroom become lower – they all go down. The class becomes calmer and it is easier to teach.

Every word counts.

There once was a young boy named Mikey. Mikey loved school. He was one of those students that every teacher wants to have. He came into the classroom with a big smile on his face excited and eager to learn. He listened to the teachers and wanted to please them. One day, his teacher got sick. Another teacher, Mrs. H, came into the classroom to teach. She gave the children a lesson and then asked them a bunch of questions. When they could not answer them, she said, "You should know this….I just taught it to you. Weren't you listening?" She called on children one by one to answer questions, and when they could not answer, she was upset with them. The children were embarrassed and frightened. Some of the students started crying. Mikey did not cry on the outside, but he cried on the inside, feeling embarrassed and dumb. It took a long time for Mikey to ever want to speak in

class again. Mrs. H. was his teacher for two months. By the time his regular teacher returned, he was convinced that he was dumb and incapable of learning. Fortunately for him, his regular teacher saw that something was very wrong. Gradually, she used her words to help Mikey believe in himself again.

I am telling you this story because every word counts. The wrong words can convince children that they are failures, and can shatter confidence. The right words can convince children that they are very capable.

Here are some words that count in a positive way when children are having a tough time "getting it."

- "I believe in you."
- "Take your time. You will get it."
- "Let me explain it another way so all of you get it."
- "You can do it."

Professional Development
"Motivate, Inspire, & Connect"
We come to you!

A sampling of ATi's most requested research-based and evidence based topics:

- How to Handle the Hard to Handle Student
- 175 Ways to Motivate the Difficult, Disruptive, Disinterested, & Defiant Student
- 109 Strategies for Differentiating Instruction
- Inclusion: Showcase for Success
- Working Effectively with Parents
- Collaborating, Co-Teaching, Teambuilding and Inclusion
- Understating and Overcoming Stress for Teachers
- The Bully Free Classroom/School
- Succeeding with Angry, O.D.D., and Aggressive Students
- Respect, Responsibility, and Character Building
- RTI - Response to Intervention — Coming Soon!!

Appelbaum Training Workshops ...
- are lead by educators with classroom experience!
- are affordable and fun!
- are easy to schedule! We do the work for you!
- are available 7 days a week!
- can be customized for your team!
- are jam packed with dozens of strategies you can implement immediately!
- can be done in full or half day sessions!
- inspire you to bring us back for more!!
- are available for multiple visit or ongoing year long implementation and consulting for your school or district!
- are **100% SATISFACTION GUARANTEED!**

Train your entire school or district . ATi in-service training = high performing classrooms with motivated staff.

CALL TODAY!!
See why ATi is rated #1 for Teacher Training
1-800-374-2291
Or go to our website at:
www.atiseminars.org

Appelbaum Training Institute

TOGETHER BUILDING BRIDGES TO THE FUTURE

Sign up to get Maryln's thoughts for the day
that inspired this book at
www.atiseminars.org

Please visit
www.teacherboutique.com
for additonal books by Maryln, gifts, and teaching aids.